D0568939

This edition published and distributed by
THE BOOK COMPANY PUBLISHING PTY LIMITED
Austlink Corporate Park, 1 Minna Close
Belrose Sydney NSW 2085 Australia

ISBN 174047032X

PUBLISHER
Glenn Johnstone

PRODUCTION MANAGER
Leslie Krey

PRODUCTION
Chris Moran, Mary Bjelobrk, Meran Gluskie and Camilla Baker

PHOTOGRAPHY
John Krey

DESIGN
Open Art Surgery

Printed in China

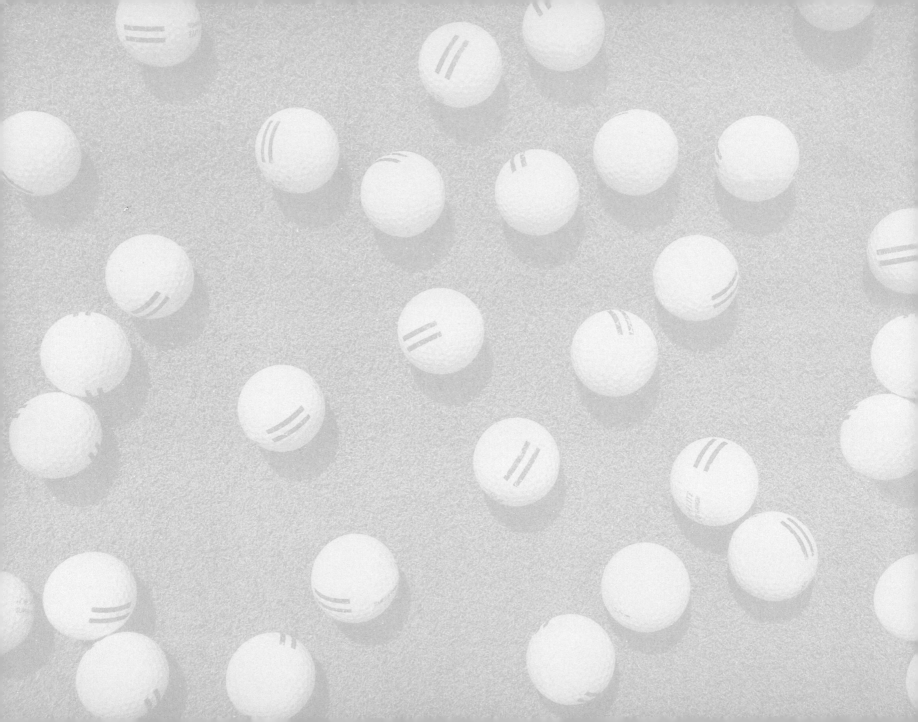

golf

RECORD BOOK

Andrew La Brooy played on the Australian tour from 1987 to 1994 taking him all around the world. Andrew represented Victoria as an amateur in 1986-87 and was selected for the Australian Amateur team in 1987.

He turned professional in 1987 and won the Victorian PGA in 1991. Andrew has been coaching since 1994 and brings a wealth of experience in the latest teaching methods to all golfers who aspire to improve their golfing skills.

INTRODUCTION

Ask yourself these questions. Do you really know your golf game? Do you know which strokes and clubs you control the ball with consistently? Most people talk about how far they hit the ball. Very rarely do you hear them speak about how well they controlled the ball, how many times they hit the fairway or how many putts they had. I see it often at club level — a high handicap golfer attempting a miracle shot, one over which even the touring professional golfer may cast doubt.

I have my father to thank for introducing me to the game of golf at the tender age of eight. When we were living in Port Moresby, I would play nine holes at the local golf course with him most days after school. This would be the beginning of my love of golf. My one and only dream was to one day defeat my father. Our competitive games led me to constantly seek his advice. His most common response was "Son, practice harder — that is the only way you will win." What should I practice? Grip, posture, irons, woods, putts, chips, bunkers? The list is endless. He encouraged me to learn and improve by targeting my weaknesses and supervising my practice.

What I learnt from an early age was the difference between playing golf and the golf swing. The difference being playing golf is simply that — "playing golf". Hit the golf ball to the target as best you can, find the ball and do it again.

The golf swing is the component you need to learn in preparation to play golf. This can be done at home, in the back yard, at the office or on the driving range, but not on the golf course — it will destroy your score.

As a golf teaching professional I spend most of my time on the driving range helping people with their golf swing. To date, not one person has come to me seeking help or advice on managing their game or analyzing their statistics to target their strengths and weaknesses. Often their swing is not the problem but rather other aspects of their game, of which they are unaware.

My advice to anyone is to keep a record of your game. How many fairways and greens you hit, how many shots you take to get the ball into the hole from a bunker, and how many putts you take for 18 holes.

Most golf instruction is aimed at repairing a person's current swing. This is not the intent of this book. By providing for a clear record of your games, the goal of this book is to pinpoint both your strengths and your weaknesses. I would then suggest visiting your local golf professional to work out a program to develop areas needing attention, according to your statistics.

Good luck and enjoy your golf!

Andrew LaBrooy

CLUB GOLF

STABLEFORD COMPETITION

The Stableford competition is the most popular event played at club level. Stableford is a game of points based on your score for each hole.

An EAGLE (two under par) scores four points

A BIRDIE (one under par) scores three points

A PAR scores two points

A BOGEY (one over par) scores one point

A DOUBLE BOGEY (two over par) or worse scores no points

In a club situation where handicaps are used, you must check the scorecard to see where each player receives strokes. You do this by using the general index/rating column.

For example, a player with an 18 handicap receives one stroke on every hole. If that player scores a bogey 5 on a par 4, he or she deducts one stroke making it a net 4 (or a net par) and the player will score two points (5-2 to appear on the scorecard). An example of how to score 3 points would be a player scores a par 4 on a par 4, minus his or her handicap shot, equals a net 3 or birdie, equals 3 points (4-3 to appear on scorecard).

Players who exceed their own par by two strokes, score no points for the hole and should pick up their ball to keep play moving. At the end of the round, all points scored are added for each nine holes and totalled for 18 holes. The player with the most points is the winner. 36 points is playing to your handicap — anything above this and you have a chance to win the day.

FOUR-BALL STABLEFORD

This game involves two players playing as partners, using the same scoring system as individual Stableford. Players retain their full handicap throughout the round, the difference being only the best Stableford score between the two players has his or her score entered on the card. Only one score is required — the score of the player who first completes the hole shall be recorded if both players score equally on the hole. The team with the most number of Stableford points after 18 holes is the winner. A great result can be achieved by having a good hole when your partner is having difficulty, and vice versa.

STROKE PLAY

Stroke is the most common type of competition played by professional golfers around the world. It is the true test of a golfer's ability as every stroke must be recorded. The method of scoring is simple. The number of strokes taken at each hole is entered onto each player's card, then totalled for each nine holes and then again for the full 18 holes. At club level using handicaps, each player's handicap is deducted from his or her gross score to give a net score. The player with the lowest net score is the winner. To win a Stroke competition you must play consistently. One or two poor holes usually proves costly and puts an end to your chances of winning.

© Digital Stock

PAR COMPETITION

Par Competition is similar to that of Stableford. It is a game based on wins, losses or halves for each hole.

A BIRDIE (one under par) or better scores a win or a "+"
A PAR scores a half or "0"
A BOGEY (one over par) or worse scores a loss or a "-"

In a club situation, where handicaps are used, you must check the scorecard to see where each player receives strokes. You do this by using the general index/rating column. For example, a player with an 18 handicap receives one stroke on every hole. If that player scores a bogey 5 on a par 4, he or she deducts one stroke making it a net 4 (or a net par), and the player will score a half or a 0 (5 0 to appear on scorecard). An example of a win or "+" would be a player scores a par 4 on a par 4, minus his or her handicap shot, equals a net 3 or birdie, equals a win or "+" (4 + to appear on scorecard).

At the end of nine holes, and the round, your score is calculated by deducting the total losses (-) from the total wins (+). The halves (0) are considered even and have no bearing on your result. The player with the highest win (+) result is the winner.

The main disadvantage of this type of competition is that if you shoot a birdie and your net result is an eagle, you gain no benefit, as you only score a win (+).

FOUR-BALL PAR

This game involves two players playing as partners using the same scoring system as individual par. Players retain their full handicap throughout the round, the difference being only the best score between the two players for each hole is recorded on the scorecard. If both players score equally on the hole, the score of the player who first completed the hole shall be recorded. Only one score is required. The team with the highest (+) result is the winner. A great result can be achieved by having a good hole when your partner is having difficulty and vice versa.

FOURSOMES

Foursomes is a stroke event played with a partner using only one golf ball. The rules require the partners to hit-off from alternate tees with alternate shots thereafter. Player A may select the even numbered holes, leaving player B to contend with the odd numbered holes. Once a player has teed off, you strike the ball alternately until the hole is completed. A team's handicap is found by adding both players' handicaps together, and then dividing the total by two. For example, 12 plus 22 = 34, divided by 2 = 17. The stroke score for each hole is on the scorecard, and totalled as in Stroke Play. The team with the lowest net score is the winner. Foursomes is fun, however you will feel the added pressure on your game to keep your shots consistent to ensure a happy partnership and a low score.

MATCH PLAY

Match Play is a game where players play against each other, hole by hole, to determine the winner. The player with the lowest score wins the particular hole, and therefore is said to be "one up" in the Match Play situation. The hole is halved if both players complete the hole with the same score. The player who is leading by a number of holes greater than the number of holes remaining, for example 5 holes up after the 14th hole with 4 holes left to play, wins the match. If your opponent wins all four holes remaining, you are still one hole up at the 18th, so the match is finished early at the 14th hole, the result being 5 and 4. In a handicap match, the lowest net score wins the hole. If there is a difference of handicaps, an eight handicap player would have to give a 19 handicap player 11 strokes. These strokes would be allocated over the eight holes according to the Match Play index on the scorecard. The bottom line is to beat your opponent's score to win the hole — birdies and pars are of no significance. Match Play has different rules to Stroke Play, and it is advisable to be familiar with these rules before entering into a match, as a mistake could cost you a hole and the match.

FOUR-BALL MATCH PLAY

This event is a popular game played at club level. It involves two teams of two players and is played under the same conditions as individual Match Play. Handicaps are worked out by making the lowest marker play off zero or scratch, and the other three handicaps are the difference between their handicap and the lowest.

For example:

	NORMAL HANDICAP	FOUR-BALL MATCH PLAY HANDICAP
Player 1	5	0
Player 2	12	7
Player 3	18	13
Player 4	26	21

Strokes are taken from the Match Play index on the scorecard. At the end of each hole the best net score for each pair determines their result. If the best net score is the same, the hole is halved. If the first pair have a lower net score than the other pair, the result is a "+" or a win, leaving the other pair with a "-" or a loss. The pair with the most "+" wins.

AMBROSE EVENTS

This is a team competition, each team comprising two to four players. It is a fun event played at most trade days where many non-golfers get the opportunity to experience golf.

The team usually selects a captain who is responsible for the order of play and the marking of the scorecard. He or she is usually the person with the lowest handicap and the most golf knowledge. All players hit-off from the tee, with the best drive being selected for the play of the second shot. All team members pick up their balls, then drop them within one club length of the selected ball no nearer the hole. They then play from this position. The same selection process is followed until the ball is holed. If the selected ball is in the rough or a hazard, the other balls must be dropped in the rough or hazard within one club length. On the putting surface all balls must be placed and putted from within 15cm of the selected ball.

Ambrose is a stroke event, with each score recorded for each hole for an 18 hole total. There are usually two winners — the first being the group with the lowest 18 hole gross total and the second being the 18 hole net winner (after deduction of handicap).

Handicaps for an Ambrose event are as follows:

TWO PERSON EVENT
both players' handicaps are added together and divided by four.
THREE PERSON EVENT
all players' handicaps are added together and divided by six.
FOUR PERSON EVENT
all players' handicaps are added together and divided by eight.

© Digital Stock

RECORDS

We have devised a simple record book of information that can be transferred from your scorecard. At the end of each round, tally the number of fairways and greens hit and the number of putts. By keeping your own records and using the graph at the end of ten games, you will be able to identify those areas of your game that need improvement.

COURSE: *Surfview Country Club* PAR: *72*
DATE: *4/2/00* WEATHER CONDITIONS: *Fine*

HOLE	PAR	SCORE	FAIRWAYS	GREENS	PUTTS	COMMENTS
1	4	4	✓	✓	2	
2	5	8	✓	X	3	Fairway Bunker X
3	4	7	X	X	2	T-shot out of bounds
4	3	4	—	✓	3	
5	4	5	X	✓	3	
6	3	5	—	X	2	
7	4	4	✓	✓	2	Great drive
8	4	5	✓	X	2	
9	5	6	✓	X	2	Missed green 9I
TOTAL	36	48	5/7	4/9	21	
10	4	5	✓	X	2	
11	4	5	X	✓	3	Missed 1m putt
12	3	4	—	X	2	
13	5	7	X	X	2	Fairway wood trees
14	4	4	✓	X	1	20ft putt
15	3	4	—	✓	3	
16	5	5	✓	✓	2	
17	4	5	X	X	2	
18	4	3	✓	✓	1	At last a one putt
TOTAL	72	90	9/14	8/18	39	

RESULT: *37pts* No. of EAGLES: *—* No. OF BIRDIES: *1*
No. OF PARS: *4* No. OF BOGIES: *9* No. OF DOUBLE BOGIES: *4*
AREAS FOR IMPROVEMENT: *Work on my long putts.*
Improve my Par 5s

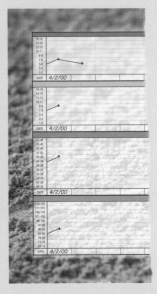

If you hit the fairway or green with your shot, tick the box. If you miss, mark with a cross. At the end of 18 holes, you will be able to ascertain your average.

COURSE: _____ PAR: _____   COURSE: _____ PAR: _____

DATE: _____ WEATHER CONDITIONS: _____   DATE: _____ WEATHER CONDITIONS: _____

HOLE	PAR	SCORE	FAIRWAYS	GREENS	PUTTS	COMMENTS
1						
2						
3						
4						
5						
6						
7						
8						
9						
TOTAL						
10						
11						
12						
13						
14						
15						
16						
17						
18						
TOTAL						

HOLE	PAR	SCORE	FAIRWAYS	GREENS	PUTTS	COMMENTS
1						
2						
3						
4						
5						
6						
7						
8						
9						
TOTAL						
10						
11						
12						
13						
14						
15						
16						
17						
18						
TOTAL						

RESULT: _____ No. of EAGLES: _____ No. OF BIRDIES: _____   RESULT: _____ No. of EAGLES: _____ No. OF BIRDIES: _____

No. OF PARS: _____ No. OF BOGIES: _____ No. OF DOUBLE BOGIES: _____   No. OF PARS: _____ No. OF BOGIES: _____ No. OF DOUBLE BOGIES: _____

AREAS FOR IMPROVEMENT: _____   AREAS FOR IMPROVEMENT: _____

| COURSE: _____ | PAR: _____ |
| DATE: _____ WEATHER CONDITIONS: _____ | |

HOLE	PAR	SCORE	FAIRWAYS	GREENS	PUTTS	COMMENTS
1						
2						
3						
4						
5						
6						
7						
8						
9						
TOTAL						
10						
11						
12						
13						
14						
15						
16						
17						
18						
TOTAL						

RESULT:_____ No. of EAGLES: _____ No. OF BIRDIES: _____

No. OF PARS: _____ No. OF BOGIES: _____ No. OF DOUBLE BOGIES: _____

AREAS FOR IMPROVEMENT: _____

| COURSE: _____ | PAR: _____ |
| DATE: _____ WEATHER CONDITIONS: _____ | |

HOLE	PAR	SCORE	FAIRWAYS	GREENS	PUTTS	COMMENTS
1						
2						
3						
4						
5						
6						
7						
8						
9						
TOTAL						
10						
11						
12						
13						
14						
15						
16						
17						
18						
TOTAL						

RESULT:_____ No. of EAGLES: _____ No. OF BIRDIES: _____

No. OF PARS: _____ No. OF BOGIES: _____ No. OF DOUBLE BOGIES: _____

AREAS FOR IMPROVEMENT: _____

COURSE: _____ PAR: _____

DATE: _____ WEATHER CONDITIONS: _____

HOLE	PAR	SCORE	FAIRWAYS	GREENS	PUTTS	COMMENTS
1						
2						
3						
4						
5						
6						
7						
8						
9						
TOTAL						
10						
11						
12						
13						
14						
15						
16						
17						
18						
TOTAL						

RESULT:_____ No. of EAGLES: _____ No. OF BIRDIES: _____

No. OF PARS: _____ No. OF BOGIES:_____ No. OF DOUBLE BOGIES: _____

AREAS FOR IMPROVEMENT: _____

_____

COURSE: _____ PAR: _____

DATE: _____ WEATHER CONDITIONS:_____

HOLE	PAR	SCORE	FAIRWAYS	GREENS	PUTTS	COMMENTS
1						
2						
3						
4						
5						
6						
7						
8						
9						
TOTAL						
10						
11						
12						
13						
14						
15						
16						
17						
18						
TOTAL						

RESULT:_____ No. of EAGLES: _____ No. OF BIRDIES: _____

No. OF PARS: _____ No. OF BOGIES:_____ No. OF DOUBLE BOGIES: _____

AREAS FOR IMPROVEMENT: _____

COURSE: _____ PAR: _____

DATE: _____ WEATHER CONDITIONS: _____

HOLE	PAR	SCORE	FAIRWAYS	GREENS	PUTTS	COMMENTS
1						
2						
3						
4						
5						
6						
7						
8						
9						
TOTAL						
10						
11						
12						
13						
14						
15						
16						
17						
18						
TOTAL						

RESULT:_____ No. of EAGLES: _____ No. OF BIRDIES: _____

No. OF PARS: _____ No. OF BOGIES: _____ No. OF DOUBLE BOGIES: _____

AREAS FOR IMPROVEMENT: _____
_____

COURSE: _____ PAR: _____

DATE: _____ WEATHER CONDITIONS: _____

HOLE	PAR	SCORE	FAIRWAYS	GREENS	PUTTS	COMMENTS
1						
2						
3						
4						
5						
6						
7						
8						
9						
TOTAL						
10						
11						
12						
13						
14						
15						
16						
17						
18						
TOTAL						

RESULT:_____ No. of EAGLES: _____ No. OF BIRDIES: _____

No. OF PARS: _____ No. OF BOGIES: _____ No. OF DOUBLE BOGIES: _____

AREAS FOR IMPROVEMENT: _____
_____

COURSE: _____ PAR: _____ COURSE: _____ PAR: _____

DATE: _____ WEATHER CONDITIONS: _____ DATE: _____ WEATHER CONDITIONS: _____

HOLE	PAR	SCORE	FAIRWAYS	GREENS	PUTTS	COMMENTS
1						
2						
3						
4						
5						
6						
7						
8						
9						
TOTAL						
10						
11						
12						
13						
14						
15						
16						
17						
18						
TOTAL						

HOLE	PAR	SCORE	FAIRWAYS	GREENS	PUTTS	COMMENTS
1						
2						
3						
4						
5						
6						
7						
8						
9						
TOTAL						
10						
11						
12						
13						
14						
15						
16						
17						
18						
TOTAL						

RESULT:_____ No. of EAGLES: _____ No. OF BIRDIES: _____ RESULT:_____ No. of EAGLES: _____ No. OF BIRDIES: _____

No. OF PARS: _____ No. OF BOGIES:_____ No. OF DOUBLE BOGIES: _____ No. OF PARS: _____ No. OF BOGIES:_____ No. OF DOUBLE BOGIES: _____

AREAS FOR IMPROVEMENT: _____ AREAS FOR IMPROVEMENT: _____

GREENS

17-18								
15-16								
13-14								
11-12								
9-10								
7-8								
5-6								
3-4								
1-2								
DATE								

FAIRWAYS

17-18								
15-16								
13-14								
11-12								
9-10								
7-8								
5-6								
3-4								
1-2								
DATE								

PUTTS

47-48								
45-46								
43-44								
41-42								
39-40								
37-38								
35-36								
33-34								
31-32								
29-30								
27-28								
25-26								
DATE								

SCORE

116-120								
111-115								
106-110								
101-105								
96-100								
91-95								
86-90								
81-85								
76-80								
71-75								
65-70								
DATE								

Posture

Having the correct posture and stance is the first step towards a good golf swing. A poor starting position will often cause a loss of power and balance.

If you wish to keep improving your golf, visit your local golf professional and start off with a lesson on grip and posture. The correct grip and posture go hand in hand. One is useless without the other.

COURSE: _____ PAR: _____

DATE: _____ WEATHER CONDITIONS:_____

HOLE	PAR	SCORE	FAIRWAYS	GREENS	PUTTS	COMMENTS
1						
2						
3						
4						
5						
6						
7						
8						
9						
TOTAL						
10						
11						
12						
13						
14						
15						
16						
17						
18						
TOTAL						

RESULT:_____ No. of EAGLES: _____ No. OF BIRDIES: _____

No. OF PARS: _____ No. OF BOGIES:_____ No. OF DOUBLE BOGIES: _____

AREAS FOR IMPROVEMENT: _____

COURSE: _____ PAR: _____

DATE: _____ WEATHER CONDITIONS:_____

HOLE	PAR	SCORE	FAIRWAYS	GREENS	PUTTS	COMMENTS
1						
2						
3						
4						
5						
6						
7						
8						
9						
TOTAL						
10						
11						
12						
13						
14						
15						
16						
17						
18						
TOTAL						

RESULT:_____ No. of EAGLES: _____ No. OF BIRDIES: _____

No. OF PARS: _____ No. OF BOGIES:_____ No. OF DOUBLE BOGIES: _____

AREAS FOR IMPROVEMENT: _____

COURSE: _____ PAR: _____   COURSE: _____ PAR: _____

DATE: _____WEATHER CONDITIONS:_____   DATE: _____WEATHER CONDITIONS:_____

HOLE	PAR	SCORE	FAIRWAYS	GREENS	PUTTS	COMMENTS
1						
2						
3						
4						
5						
6						
7						
8						
9						
TOTAL						
10						
11						
12						
13						
14						
15						
16						
17						
18						
TOTAL						

HOLE	PAR	SCORE	FAIRWAYS	GREENS	PUTTS	COMMENTS
1						
2						
3						
4						
5						
6						
7						
8						
9						
TOTAL						
10						
11						
12						
13						
14						
15						
16						
17						
18						
TOTAL						

RESULT:_____ No. of EAGLES: _____ No. OF BIRDIES: _____   RESULT:_____ No. of EAGLES: _____ No. OF BIRDIES: _____

No. OF PARS: _____ No. OF BOGIES:_____ No. OF DOUBLE BOGIES: _____   No. OF PARS: _____ No. OF BOGIES:_____ No. OF DOUBLE BOGIES: _____

AREAS FOR IMPROVEMENT: _____   AREAS FOR IMPROVEMENT: _____

_____   _____

COURSE: _____ PAR: _____   COURSE: _____ PAR: _____

DATE: _____ WEATHER CONDITIONS: _____   DATE: _____ WEATHER CONDITIONS: _____

HOLE	PAR	SCORE	FAIRWAYS	GREENS	PUTTS	COMMENTS
1						
2						
3						
4						
5						
6						
7						
8						
9						
TOTAL						
10						
11						
12						
13						
14						
15						
16						
17						
18						
TOTAL						

HOLE	PAR	SCORE	FAIRWAYS	GREENS	PUTTS	COMMENTS
1						
2						
3						
4						
5						
6						
7						
8						
9						
TOTAL						
10						
11						
12						
13						
14						
15						
16						
17						
18						
TOTAL						

RESULT: _____ No. of EAGLES: _____ No. OF BIRDIES: _____   RESULT: _____ No. of EAGLES: _____ No. OF BIRDIES: _____

No. OF PARS: _____ No. OF BOGIES: _____ No. OF DOUBLE BOGIES: _____   No. OF PARS: _____ No. OF BOGIES: _____ No. OF DOUBLE BOGIES: _____

AREAS FOR IMPROVEMENT: _____   AREAS FOR IMPROVEMENT: _____

_____   _____

COURSE: _____ PAR: _____   COURSE: _____ PAR: _____

DATE: _____ WEATHER CONDITIONS: _____   DATE: _____ WEATHER CONDITIONS: _____

HOLE	PAR	SCORE	FAIRWAYS	GREENS	PUTTS	COMMENTS
1						
2						
3						
4						
5						
6						
7						
8						
9						
TOTAL						
10						
11						
12						
13						
14						
15						
16						
17						
18						
TOTAL						

HOLE	PAR	SCORE	FAIRWAYS	GREENS	PUTTS	COMMENTS
1						
2						
3						
4						
5						
6						
7						
8						
9						
TOTAL						
10						
11						
12						
13						
14						
15						
16						
17						
18						
TOTAL						

RESULT:_____ No. of EAGLES: _____ No. OF BIRDIES: _____   RESULT:_____ No. of EAGLES: _____ No. OF BIRDIES: _____

No. OF PARS: _____ No. OF BOGIES:_____ No. OF DOUBLE BOGIES: _____   No. OF PARS: _____ No. OF BOGIES:_____ No. OF DOUBLE BOGIES: _____

AREAS FOR IMPROVEMENT: _____   AREAS FOR IMPROVEMENT: _____

COURSE: _____ PAR: _____   COURSE: _____ PAR: _____

DATE: _____ WEATHER CONDITIONS: _____   DATE: _____ WEATHER CONDITIONS: _____

HOLE	PAR	SCORE	FAIRWAYS	GREENS	PUTTS	COMMENTS
1						
2						
3						
4						
5						
6						
7						
8						
9						
TOTAL						
10						
11						
12						
13						
14						
15						
16						
17						
18						
TOTAL						

HOLE	PAR	SCORE	FAIRWAYS	GREENS	PUTTS	COMMENTS
1						
2						
3						
4						
5						
6						
7						
8						
9						
TOTAL						
10						
11						
12						
13						
14						
15						
16						
17						
18						
TOTAL						

RESULT:_____ No. of EAGLES: _____ No. OF BIRDIES: _____   RESULT:_____ No. of EAGLES: _____ No. OF BIRDIES: _____

No. OF PARS: _____ No. OF BOGIES:_____ No. OF DOUBLE BOGIES: _____   No. OF PARS: _____ No. OF BOGIES:_____ No. OF DOUBLE BOGIES: _____

AREAS FOR IMPROVEMENT: _____   AREAS FOR IMPROVEMENT: _____

GREENS

17-18									
15-16									
13-14									
11-12									
9-10									
7-8									
5-6									
3-4									
1-2									
DATE									

FAIRWAYS

17-18									
15-16									
13-14									
11-12									
9-10									
7-8									
5-6									
3-4									
1-2									
DATE									

PUTTS

47-48									
45-46									
43-44									
41-42									
39-40									
37-30									
35-36									
33-34									
31-32									
29-30									
27-28									
25-26									
DATE									

SCORE

116-120									
111-115									
106-110									
101-105									
96 100									
91-95									
86-90									
81-85									
76-80									
71-75									
65-70									
DATE									

COURSE: _____ PAR: _____

DATE: _____ WEATHER CONDITIONS: _____

HOLE	PAR	SCORE	FAIRWAYS	GREENS	PUTTS	COMMENTS
1						
2						
3						
4						
5						
6						
7						
8						
9						
TOTAL						
10						
11						
12						
13						
14						
15						
16						
17						
18						
TOTAL						

RESULT:_____ No. of EAGLES: _____ No. OF BIRDIES: _____

No. OF PARS: _____ No. OF BOGIES:_____ No. OF DOUBLE BOGIES: _____

AREAS FOR IMPROVEMENT: _____

_____

COURSE: _____ PAR: _____

DATE: _____ WEATHER CONDITIONS: _____

HOLE	PAR	SCORE	FAIRWAYS	GREENS	PUTTS	COMMENTS
1						
2						
3						
4						
5						
6						
7						
8						
9						
TOTAL						
10						
11						
12						
13						
14						
15						
16						
17						
18						
TOTAL						

RESULT:_____ No. of EAGLES: _____ No. OF BIRDIES: _____

No. OF PARS: _____ No. OF BOGIES:_____ No. OF DOUBLE BOGIES: _____

AREAS FOR IMPROVEMENT: _____

_____

COURSE: _____ PAR: _____   COURSE: _____ PAR: _____

DATE: _____ WEATHER CONDITIONS: _____   DATE: _____ WEATHER CONDITIONS: _____

HOLE	PAR	SCORE	FAIRWAYS	GREENS	PUTTS	COMMENTS
1						
2						
3						
4						
5						
6						
7						
8						
9						
TOTAL						
10						
11						
12						
13						
14						
15						
16						
17						
18						
TOTAL						

HOLE	PAR	SCORE	FAIRWAYS	GREENS	PUTTS	COMMENTS
1						
2						
3						
4						
5						
6						
7						
8						
9						
TOTAL						
10						
11						
12						
13						
14						
15						
16						
17						
18						
TOTAL						

RESULT: _____ No. of EAGLES: _____ No. OF BIRDIES: _____   RESULT: _____ No. of EAGLES: _____ No. OF BIRDIES: _____

No. OF PARS: _____ No. OF BOGIES: _____ No. OF DOUBLE BOGIES: _____   No. OF PARS: _____ No. OF BOGIES: _____ No. OF DOUBLE BOGIES: _____

AREAS FOR IMPROVEMENT: _____   AREAS FOR IMPROVEMENT: _____

COURSE: _____ PAR: _____

DATE: _____ WEATHER CONDITIONS: _____

HOLE	PAR	SCORE	FAIRWAYS	GREENS	PUTTS	COMMENTS
1						
2						
3						
4						
5						
6						
7						
8						
9						
TOTAL						
10						
11						
12						
13						
14						
15						
16						
17						
18						
TOTAL						

RESULT:_____ No. of EAGLES: _____ No. OF BIRDIES: _____

No. OF PARS: _____ No. OF BOGIES:_____ No. OF DOUBLE BOGIES: _____

AREAS FOR IMPROVEMENT: _____

COURSE: _____ PAR: _____

DATE: _____ WEATHER CONDITIONS: _____

HOLE	PAR	SCORE	FAIRWAYS	GREENS	PUTTS	COMMENTS
1						
2						
3						
4						
5						
6						
7						
8						
9						
TOTAL						
10						
11						
12						
13						
14						
15						
16						
17						
18						
TOTAL						

RESULT:_____ No. of EAGLES: _____ No. OF BIRDIES: _____

No. OF PARS: _____ No. OF BOGIES:_____ No. OF DOUBLE BOGIES: _____

AREAS FOR IMPROVEMENT: _____

HOLE	PAR	SCORE	FAIRWAYS	GREENS	PUTTS	COMMENTS
1						
2						
3						
4						
5						
6						
7						
8						
9						
TOTAL						
10						
11						
12						
13						
14						
15						
16						
17						
18						
TOTAL						

COURSE: _____ PAR: _____

DATE: _____ WEATHER CONDITIONS: _____

RESULT:_____ No. of EAGLES: _____ No. OF BIRDIES: _____

No. OF PARS: _____ No. OF BOGIES:_____ No. OF DOUBLE BOGIES: _____

AREAS FOR IMPROVEMENT: _____

_____

HOLE	PAR	SCORE	FAIRWAYS	GREENS	PUTTS	COMMENTS
1						
2						
3						
4						
5						
6						
7						
8						
9						
TOTAL						
10						
11						
12						
13						
14						
15						
16						
17						
18						
TOTAL						

COURSE: _____ PAR: _____

DATE: _____ WEATHER CONDITIONS: _____

RESULT:_____ No. of EAGLES: _____ No. OF BIRDIES: _____

No. OF PARS: _____ No. OF BOGIES:_____ No. OF DOUBLE BOGIES: _____

AREAS FOR IMPROVEMENT: _____

_____

COURSE: _____ PAR: _____

DATE: _____ WEATHER CONDITIONS: _____

HOLE	PAR	SCORE	FAIRWAYS	GREENS	PUTTS	COMMENTS
1						
2						
3						
4						
5						
6						
7						
8						
9						
TOTAL						
10						
11						
12						
13						
14						
15						
16						
17						
18						
TOTAL						

RESULT:_____ No. of EAGLES: _____ No. OF BIRDIES: _____

No. OF PARS: _____ No. OF BOGIES:_____ No. OF DOUBLE BOGIES: _____

AREAS FOR IMPROVEMENT: _____

_____

COURSE: _____ PAR: _____

DATE: _____ WEATHER CONDITIONS: _____

HOLE	PAR	SCORE	FAIRWAYS	GREENS	PUTTS	COMMENTS
1						
2						
3						
4						
5						
6						
7						
8						
9						
TOTAL						
10						
11						
12						
13						
14						
15						
16						
17						
18						
TOTAL						

RESULT:_____ No. of EAGLES: _____ No. OF BIRDIES: _____

No. OF PARS: _____ No. OF BOGIES:_____ No. OF DOUBLE BOGIES: _____

AREAS FOR IMPROVEMENT: _____

_____

GREENS

17-18									
15-16									
13-14									
11-12									
9-10									
7-8									
5-6									
3-4									
1-2									
DATE									

FAIRWAYS

17-18									
15-16									
13-14									
11-12									
9-10									
7-8									
5-6									
3-4									
1-2									
DATE									

PUTTS

47-48									
45-46									
43-44									
41-42									
39-40									
37-38									
35-36									
33-34									
31-32									
29-30									
27-28									
25-26									
DATE									

SCORE

116-120									
111-115									
106-110									
101-105									
96-100									
91-95									
86-90									
81-85									
76-80									
71-75									
65-70									
DATE									

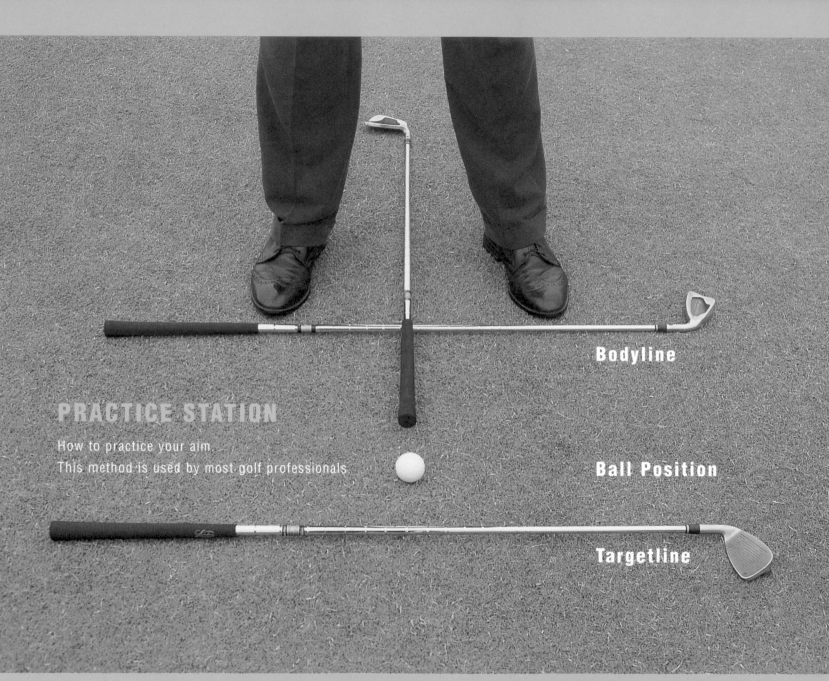

Bodyline

PRACTICE STATION

How to practice your aim.
This method is used by most golf professionals.

Ball Position

Targetline

POSITIONING
OF FEET

Don't make the mistake that most golfers make by aiming their feet and body at the target. Feet should be positioned parallel to the target. Shoulders, hips, knees and feet are all square.

Bodyline

Targetline

| COURSE: _____ PAR: _____ |
| DATE: _____ WEATHER CONDITIONS: _____ |

HOLE	PAR	SCORE	FAIRWAYS	GREENS	PUTTS	COMMENTS
1						
2						
3						
4						
5						
6						
7						
8						
9						
TOTAL						
10						
11						
12						
13						
14						
15						
16						
17						
18						
TOTAL						

RESULT:_____ No. of EAGLES: _____ No. OF BIRDIES: _____

No. OF PARS: _____ No. OF BOGIES:_____ No. OF DOUBLE BOGIES: _____

AREAS FOR IMPROVEMENT: _____

| COURSE: _____ PAR: _____ |
| DATE: _____ WEATHER CONDITIONS: _____ |

HOLE	PAR	SCORE	FAIRWAYS	GREENS	PUTTS	COMMENTS
1						
2						
3						
4						
5						
6						
7						
8						
9						
TOTAL						
10						
11						
12						
13						
14						
15						
16						
17						
18						
TOTAL						

RESULT:_____ No. of EAGLES: _____ No. OF BIRDIES: _____

No. OF PARS: _____ No. OF BOGIES:_____ No. OF DOUBLE BOGIES: _____

AREAS FOR IMPROVEMENT: _____

COURSE: _____ PAR: _____

DATE: _____ WEATHER CONDITIONS: _____

HOLE	PAR	SCORE	FAIRWAYS	GREENS	PUTTS	COMMENTS
1						
2						
3						
4						
5						
6						
7						
8						
9						
TOTAL						
10						
11						
12						
13						
14						
15						
16						
17						
18						
TOTAL						

RESULT:_____ No. of EAGLES: _____ No. OF BIRDIES: _____

No. OF PARS: _____ No. OF BOGIES:_____ No. OF DOUBLE BOGIES: _____

AREAS FOR IMPROVEMENT: _____

COURSE: _____ PAR: _____

DATE: _____ WEATHER CONDITIONS: _____

HOLE	PAR	SCORE	FAIRWAYS	GREENS	PUTTS	COMMENTS
1						
2						
3						
4						
5						
6						
7						
8						
9						
TOTAL						
10						
11						
12						
13						
14						
15						
16						
17						
18						
TOTAL						

RESULT:_____ No. of EAGLES: _____ No. OF BIRDIES: _____

No. OF PARS: _____ No. OF BOGIES:_____ No. OF DOUBLE BOGIES: _____

AREAS FOR IMPROVEMENT: _____

COURSE: _____ PAR: _____   COURSE: _____ PAR: _____

DATE: _____ WEATHER CONDITIONS: _____   DATE: _____ WEATHER CONDITIONS: _____

HOLE	PAR	SCORE	FAIRWAYS	GREENS	PUTTS	COMMENTS
1						
2						
3						
4						
5						
6						
7						
8						
9						
TOTAL						
10						
11						
12						
13						
14						
15						
16						
17						
18						
TOTAL						

HOLE	PAR	SCORE	FAIRWAYS	GREENS	PUTTS	COMMENTS
1						
2						
3						
4						
5						
6						
7						
8						
9						
TOTAL						
10						
11						
12						
13						
14						
15						
16						
17						
18						
TOTAL						

RESULT:_____ No. of EAGLES: _____ No. OF BIRDIES: _____   RESULT:_____ No. of EAGLES: _____ No. OF BIRDIES: _____

No. OF PARS: _____ No. OF BOGIES:_____ No. OF DOUBLE BOGIES: _____   No. OF PARS: _____ No. OF BOGIES:_____ No. OF DOUBLE BOGIES: _____

AREAS FOR IMPROVEMENT: _____   AREAS FOR IMPROVEMENT: _____

COURSE: _____ PAR: _____   COURSE: _____ PAR: _____

DATE: _____ WEATHER CONDITIONS: _____   DATE: _____ WEATHER CONDITIONS: _____

HOLE	PAR	SCORE	FAIRWAYS	GREENS	PUTTS	COMMENTS
1						
2						
3						
4						
5						
6						
7						
8						
9						
TOTAL						
10						
11						
12						
13						
14						
15						
16						
17						
18						
TOTAL						

HOLE	PAR	SCORE	FAIRWAYS	GREENS	PUTTS	COMMENTS
1						
2						
3						
4						
5						
6						
7						
8						
9						
TOTAL						
10						
11						
12						
13						
14						
15						
16						
17						
18						
TOTAL						

RESULT: _____ No. of EAGLES: _____ No. OF BIRDIES: _____   RESULT: _____ No. of EAGLES: _____ No. OF BIRDIES: _____

No. OF PARS: _____ No. OF BOGIES: _____ No. OF DOUBLE BOGIES: _____   No. OF PARS: _____ No. OF BOGIES: _____ No. OF DOUBLE BOGIES: _____

AREAS FOR IMPROVEMENT: _____   AREAS FOR IMPROVEMENT: _____

COURSE: _____ PAR: _____   COURSE: _____ PAR: _____

DATE: _____ WEATHER CONDITIONS: _____   DATE: _____ WEATHER CONDITIONS: _____

HOLE	PAR	SCORE	FAIRWAYS	GREENS	PUTTS	COMMENTS
1						
2						
3						
4						
5						
6						
7						
8						
9						
TOTAL						
10						
11						
12						
13						
14						
15						
16						
17						
18						
TOTAL						

HOLE	PAR	SCORE	FAIRWAYS	GREENS	PUTTS	COMMENTS
1						
2						
3						
4						
5						
6						
7						
8						
9						
TOTAL						
10						
11						
12						
13						
14						
15						
16						
17						
18						
TOTAL						

RESULT:_____ No. of EAGLES: _____ No. OF BIRDIES: _____   RESULT:_____ No. of EAGLES: _____ No. OF BIRDIES: _____

No. OF PARS: _____ No. OF BOGIES:_____ No. OF DOUBLE BOGIES: _____   No. OF PARS: _____ No. OF BOGIES:_____ No. OF DOUBLE BOGIES: _____

AREAS FOR IMPROVEMENT: _____   AREAS FOR IMPROVEMENT: _____

GREENS

17-18								
15-16								
13-14								
11-12								
9-10								
7-8								
5-6								
3-4								
1-2								
DATE								

FAIRWAYS

17-18								
15-16								
13-14								
11-12								
9-10								
7-8								
5-6								
3-4								
1-2								
DATE								

PUTTS

47-48								
45-46								
43-44								
41-42								
39-40								
37-38								
35-36								
33-34								
31-32								
29-30								
27-28								
25-26								
DATE								

SCORE

116-120								
111-115								
106-110								
101-105								
96-100								
91-95								
86-90								
81-85								
76-80								
71-75								
65-70								
DATE								

COURSE: _____ PAR: _____   COURSE: _____ PAR: _____

DATE: _____ WEATHER CONDITIONS: _____   DATE: _____ WEATHER CONDITIONS: _____

HOLE	PAR	SCORE	FAIRWAYS	GREENS	PUTTS	COMMENTS
1						
2						
3						
4						
5						
6						
7						
8						
9						
TOTAL						
10						
11						
12						
13						
14						
15						
16						
17						
18						
TOTAL						

HOLE	PAR	SCORE	FAIRWAYS	GREENS	PUTTS	COMMENTS
1						
2						
3						
4						
5						
6						
7						
8						
9						
TOTAL						
10						
11						
12						
13						
14						
15						
16						
17						
18						
TOTAL						

RESULT: _____ No. of EAGLES: _____ No. OF BIRDIES: _____   RESULT: _____ No. of EAGLES: _____ No. OF BIRDIES: _____

No. OF PARS: _____ No. OF BOGIES: _____ No. OF DOUBLE BOGIES: _____   No. OF PARS: _____ No. OF BOGIES: _____ No. OF DOUBLE BOGIES: _____

AREAS FOR IMPROVEMENT: _____   AREAS FOR IMPROVEMENT: _____

COURSE: _____ PAR: _____   COURSE: _____ PAR: _____

DATE: _____ WEATHER CONDITIONS: _____   DATE: _____ WEATHER CONDITIONS: _____

HOLE	PAR	SCORE	FAIRWAYS	GREENS	PUTTS	COMMENTS
1						
2						
3						
4						
5						
6						
7						
8						
9						
TOTAL						
10						
11						
12						
13						
14						
15						
16						
17						
18						
TOTAL						

HOLE	PAR	SCORE	FAIRWAYS	GREENS	PUTTS	COMMENTS
1						
2						
3						
4						
5						
6						
7						
8						
9						
TOTAL						
10						
11						
12						
13						
14						
15						
16						
17						
18						
TOTAL						

RESULT:_____ No. of EAGLES: _____ No. OF BIRDIES: _____

No. OF PARS: _____ No. OF BOGIES:_____ No. OF DOUBLE BOGIES: _____

AREAS FOR IMPROVEMENT: _____

RESULT:_____ No. of EAGLES: _____ No. OF BIRDIES: _____

No. OF PARS: _____ No. OF BOGIES:_____ No. OF DOUBLE BOGIES: _____

AREAS FOR IMPROVEMENT: _____

COURSE: _____ PAR: _____

DATE: _____ WEATHER CONDITIONS: _____

HOLE	PAR	SCORE	FAIRWAYS	GREENS	PUTTS	COMMENTS
1						
2						
3						
4						
5						
6						
7						
8						
9						
TOTAL						
10						
11						
12						
13						
14						
15						
16						
17						
18						
TOTAL						

RESULT:_____ No. of EAGLES: _____ No. OF BIRDIES: _____

No. OF PARS: _____ No. OF BOGIES: _____ No. OF DOUBLE BOGIES: _____

AREAS FOR IMPROVEMENT: _____

COURSE: _____ PAR: _____

DATE: _____ WEATHER CONDITIONS: _____

HOLE	PAR	SCORE	FAIRWAYS	GREENS	PUTTS	COMMENTS
1						
2						
3						
4						
5						
6						
7						
8						
9						
TOTAL						
10						
11						
12						
13						
14						
15						
16						
17						
18						
TOTAL						

RESULT:_____ No. of EAGLES: _____ No. OF BIRDIES: _____

No. OF PARS: _____ No. OF BOGIES: _____ No. OF DOUBLE BOGIES: _____

AREAS FOR IMPROVEMENT: _____

COURSE: _____ PAR: _____   COURSE: _____ PAR: _____

DATE: _____ WEATHER CONDITIONS: _____   DATE: _____ WEATHER CONDITIONS: _____

HOLE	PAR	SCORE	FAIRWAYS	GREENS	PUTTS	COMMENTS
1						
2						
3						
4						
5						
6						
7						
8						
9						
TOTAL						
10						
11						
12						
13						
14						
15						
16						
17						
18						
TOTAL						

HOLE	PAR	SCORE	FAIRWAYS	GREENS	PUTTS	COMMENTS
1						
2						
3						
4						
5						
6						
7						
8						
9						
TOTAL						
10						
11						
12						
13						
14						
15						
16						
17						
18						
TOTAL						

RESULT:_____ No. of EAGLES: _____ No. OF BIRDIES: _____   RESULT:_____ No. of EAGLES: _____ No. OF BIRDIES: _____

No. OF PARS: _____ No. OF BOGIES:_____ No. OF DOUBLE BOGIES: _____   No. OF PARS: _____ No. OF BOGIES:_____ No. OF DOUBLE BOGIES: _____

AREAS FOR IMPROVEMENT: _____   AREAS FOR IMPROVEMENT: _____

COURSE: _____ PAR: _____   COURSE: _____ PAR: _____

DATE: _____ WEATHER CONDITIONS: _____   DATE: _____ WEATHER CONDITIONS: _____

HOLE	PAR	SCORE	FAIRWAYS	GREENS	PUTTS	COMMENTS
1						
2						
3						
4						
5						
6						
7						
8						
9						
TOTAL						
10						
11						
12						
13						
14						
15						
16						
17						
18						
TOTAL						

HOLE	PAR	SCORE	FAIRWAYS	GREENS	PUTTS	COMMENTS
1						
2						
3						
4						
5						
6						
7						
8						
9						
TOTAL						
10						
11						
12						
13						
14						
15						
16						
17						
18						
TOTAL						

RESULT:_____ No. of EAGLES: _____ No. OF BIRDIES: _____   RESULT:_____ No. of EAGLES: _____ No. OF BIRDIES: _____

No. OF PARS: _____ No. OF BOGIES: _____ No. OF DOUBLE BOGIES: _____   No. OF PARS: _____ No. OF BOGIES: _____ No. OF DOUBLE BOGIES: _____

AREAS FOR IMPROVEMENT: _____   AREAS FOR IMPROVEMENT: _____

GREENS

17-18										
15-16										
13-14										
11-12										
9-10										
7-8										
5-6										
3-4										
1-2										
DATE										

FAIRWAYS

17-18										
15-16										
13-14										
11-12										
9-10										
7-8										
5 6										
3-4										
1-2										
DATE										

PUTTS

47-48										
45-46										
43-44										
41-42										
39-40										
37-38										
35-36										
33-34										
31-32										
29-30										
27-28										
25-26										
DATE										

SCORE

116-120										
111-115										
106-110										
101-105										
96-100										
91-95										
86-90										
81-85										
76-80										
71-75										
65-70										
DATE										

HITTING ONTO A TOWEL

Control the distance your ball travels in the air
by trying to land your chip shots onto a towel.
Change clubs, paying attention to ball trajectory
and run.

HITTING ONTO
THE GREEN

When assessing a chip, you need to
consider the terrain between your ball
and the hole for hardness, wind slope
and the lie of the ball.

The safe option, if you have a bunker
between yourself and the green, would be to hit
to the left of the pin. Play within your limitation,
don't be greedy and take risks.

COURSE: _____ PAR: _____

DATE: _____ WEATHER CONDITIONS: _____

HOLE	PAR	SCORE	FAIRWAYS	GREENS	PUTTS	COMMENTS
1						
2						
3						
4						
5						
6						
7						
8						
9						
TOTAL						
10						
11						
12						
13						
14						
15						
16						
17						
18						
TOTAL						

RESULT: _____ No. of EAGLES: _____ No. OF BIRDIES: _____

No. OF PARS: _____ No. OF BOGIES: _____ No. OF DOUBLE BOGIES: _____

AREAS FOR IMPROVEMENT: _____

_____

COURSE: _____ PAR: _____

DATE: _____ WEATHER CONDITIONS: _____

HOLE	PAR	SCORE	FAIRWAYS	GREENS	PUTTS	COMMENTS
1						
2						
3						
4						
5						
6						
7						
8						
9						
TOTAL						
10						
11						
12						
13						
14						
15						
16						
17						
18						
TOTAL						

RESULT: _____ No. of EAGLES: _____ No. OF BIRDIES: _____

No. OF PARS: _____ No. OF BOGIES: _____ No. OF DOUBLE BOGIES: _____

AREAS FOR IMPROVEMENT: _____

_____

COURSE: _____ PAR: _____

DATE: _____ WEATHER CONDITIONS: _____

HOLE	PAR	SCORE	FAIRWAYS	GREENS	PUTTS	COMMENTS
1						
2						
3						
4						
5						
6						
7						
8						
9						
TOTAL						
10						
11						
12						
13						
14						
15						
16						
17						
18						
TOTAL						

RESULT:_____ No. of EAGLES: _____ No. OF BIRDIES: _____

No. OF PARS: _____ No. OF BOGIES:_____ No. OF DOUBLE BOGIES: _____

AREAS FOR IMPROVEMENT: _____

_____

COURSE: _____ PAR: _____

DATE: _____ WEATHER CONDITIONS: _____

HOLE	PAR	SCORE	FAIRWAYS	GREENS	PUTTS	COMMENTS
1						
2						
3						
4						
5						
6						
7						
8						
9						
TOTAL						
10						
11						
12						
13						
14						
15						
16						
17						
18						
TOTAL						

RESULT:_____ No. of EAGLES: _____ No. OF BIRDIES: _____

No. OF PARS: _____ No. OF BOGIES:_____ No. OF DOUBLE BOGIES: _____

AREAS FOR IMPROVEMENT: _____

COURSE: _____ PAR: _____

DATE: _____ WEATHER CONDITIONS:_____

HOLE	PAR	SCORE	FAIRWAYS	GREENS	PUTTS	COMMENTS
1						
2						
3						
4						
5						
6						
7						
8						
9						
TOTAL						
10						
11						
12						
13						
14						
15						
16						
17						
18						
TOTAL						

RESULT:_____ No. of EAGLES: _____ No. OF BIRDIES: _____

No. OF PARS: _____ No. OF BOGIES:_____ No. OF DOUBLE BOGIES: _____

AREAS FOR IMPROVEMENT: _____

COURSE: _____ PAR: _____

DATE: _____ WEATHER CONDITIONS:_____

HOLE	PAR	SCORE	FAIRWAYS	GREENS	PUTTS	COMMENTS
1						
2						
3						
4						
5						
6						
7						
8						
9						
TOTAL						
10						
11						
12						
13						
14						
15						
16						
17						
18						
TOTAL						

RESULT:_____ No. of EAGLES: _____ No. OF BIRDIES: _____

No. OF PARS: _____ No. OF BOGIES:_____ No. OF DOUBLE BOGIES: _____

AREAS FOR IMPROVEMENT: _____

COURSE: _____ PAR: _____

DATE: _____ WEATHER CONDITIONS: _____

HOLE	PAR	SCORE	FAIRWAYS	GREENS	PUTTS	COMMENTS
1						
2						
3						
4						
5						
6						
7						
8						
9						
TOTAL						
10						
11						
12						
13						
14						
15						
16						
17						
18						
TOTAL						

RESULT: _____ No. of EAGLES: _____ No. OF BIRDIES: _____

No. OF PARS: _____ No. OF BOGIES: _____ No. OF DOUBLE BOGIES: _____

AREAS FOR IMPROVEMENT: _____

COURSE: _____ PAR: _____

DATE: _____ WEATHER CONDITIONS: _____

HOLE	PAR	SCORE	FAIRWAYS	GREENS	PUTTS	COMMENTS
1						
2						
3						
4						
5						
6						
7						
8						
9						
TOTAL						
10						
11						
12						
13						
14						
15						
16						
17						
18						
TOTAL						

RESULT: _____ No. of EAGLES: _____ No. OF BIRDIES: _____

No. OF PARS: _____ No. OF BOGIES: _____ No. OF DOUBLE BOGIES: _____

AREAS FOR IMPROVEMENT: _____

COURSE: _____ PAR: _____   COURSE: _____ PAR: _____

DATE: _____ WEATHER CONDITIONS: _____   DATE: _____ WEATHER CONDITIONS: _____

HOLE	PAR	SCORE	FAIRWAYS	GREENS	PUTTS	COMMENTS
1						
2						
3						
4						
5						
6						
7						
8						
9						
TOTAL						
10						
11						
12						
13						
14						
15						
16						
17						
18						
TOTAL						

HOLE	PAR	SCORE	FAIRWAYS	GREENS	PUTTS	COMMENTS
1						
2						
3						
4						
5						
6						
7						
8						
9						
TOTAL						
10						
11						
12						
13						
14						
15						
16						
17						
18						
TOTAL						

RESULT:_____ No. of EAGLES: _____ No. OF BIRDIES: _____   RESULT:_____ No. of EAGLES: _____ No. OF BIRDIES: _____

No. OF PARS: _____ No. OF BOGIES: _____ No. OF DOUBLE BOGIES: _____   No. OF PARS: _____ No. OF BOGIES: _____ No. OF DOUBLE BOGIES: _____

AREAS FOR IMPROVEMENT: _____   AREAS FOR IMPROVEMENT: _____

GREENS

17-18									
15-16									
13-14									
11-12									
9-10									
7-8									
5-6									
3-4									
1-2									
DATE									

FAIRWAYS

17-18									
15-16									
13-14									
11-12									
9-10									
7-8									
5-6									
3-4									
1-2									
DATE									

PUTTS

47-48									
45-46									
43-44									
41-42									
39-40									
37-38									
35-36									
33-34									
31-32									
29-30									
27-28									
25-26									
DATE									

SCORE

116-120									
111-115									
106-110									
101-105									
96-100									
91-95									
86-90									
81-85									
76-80									
71-75									
65-70									
DATE									

COURSE: _____ PAR: _____

DATE: _____ WEATHER CONDITIONS:_____

HOLE	PAR	SCORE	FAIRWAYS	GREENS	PUTTS	COMMENTS
1						
2						
3						
4						
5						
6						
7						
8						
9						
TOTAL						
10						
11						
12						
13						
14						
15						
16						
17						
18						
TOTAL						

RESULT:_____ No. of EAGLES: _____ No. OF BIRDIES:_____

No. OF PARS: _____ No. OF BOGIES:_____ No. OF DOUBLE BOGIES: _____

AREAS FOR IMPROVEMENT: _____
_____

COURSE: _____ PAR: _____

DATE: _____ WEATHER CONDITIONS:_____

HOLE	PAR	SCORE	FAIRWAYS	GREENS	PUTTS	COMMENTS
1						
2						
3						
4						
5						
6						
7						
8						
9						
TOTAL						
10						
11						
12						
13						
14						
15						
16						
17						
18						
TOTAL						

RESULT:_____ No. of EAGLES: _____ No. OF BIRDIES:_____

No. OF PARS: _____ No. OF BOGIES:_____ No. OF DOUBLE BOGIES: _____

AREAS FOR IMPROVEMENT: _____
_____

COURSE: _____					PAR: _____

DATE: _____ WEATHER CONDITIONS:_____

HOLE	PAR	SCORE	FAIRWAYS	GREENS	PUTTS	COMMENTS
1						
2						
3						
4						
5						
6						
7						
8						
9						
TOTAL						
10						
11						
12						
13						
14						
15						
16						
17						
18						
TOTAL						

RESULT:_____ No. of EAGLES: _____ No. OF BIRDIES: _____

No. OF PARS: _____ No. OF BOGIES:_____ No. OF DOUBLE BOGIES: _____

AREAS FOR IMPROVEMENT: _____

COURSE: _____					PAR: _____

DATE: _____ WEATHER CONDITIONS:_____

HOLE	PAR	SCORE	FAIRWAYS	GREENS	PUTTS	COMMENTS
1						
2						
3						
4						
5						
6						
7						
8						
9						
TOTAL						
10						
11						
12						
13						
14						
15						
16						
17						
18						
TOTAL						

RESULT:_____ No. of EAGLES: _____ No. OF BIRDIES: _____

No. OF PARS: _____ No. OF BOGIES:_____ No. OF DOUBLE BOGIES: _____

AREAS FOR IMPROVEMENT: _____

COURSE: _____ PAR: _____ COURSE: _____ PAR: _____

DATE: _____ WEATHER CONDITIONS: _____ DATE: _____ WEATHER CONDITIONS: _____

HOLE	PAR	SCORE	FAIRWAYS	GREENS	PUTTS	COMMENTS
1						
2						
3						
4						
5						
6						
7						
8						
9						
TOTAL						
10						
11						
12						
13						
14						
15						
16						
17						
18						
TOTAL						

HOLE	PAR	SCORE	FAIRWAYS	GREENS	PUTTS	COMMENTS
1						
2						
3						
4						
5						
6						
7						
8						
9						
TOTAL						
10						
11						
12						
13						
14						
15						
16						
17						
18						
TOTAL						

RESULT: _____ No. of EAGLES: _____ No. OF BIRDIES: _____

No. OF PARS: _____ No. OF BOGIES: _____ No. OF DOUBLE BOGIES: _____

AREAS FOR IMPROVEMENT: _____

RESULT: _____ No. of EAGLES: _____ No. OF BIRDIES: _____

No. OF PARS: _____ No. OF BOGIES: _____ No. OF DOUBLE BOGIES: _____

AREAS FOR IMPROVEMENT: _____

COURSE: _____ PAR: _____   COURSE: _____ PAR: _____

DATE: _____ WEATHER CONDITIONS: _____   DATE: _____ WEATHER CONDITIONS: _____

HOLE	PAR	SCORE	FAIRWAYS	GREENS	PUTTS	COMMENTS
1						
2						
3						
4						
5						
6						
7						
8						
9						
TOTAL						
10						
11						
12						
13						
14						
15						
16						
17						
18						
TOTAL						

HOLE	PAR	SCORE	FAIRWAYS	GREENS	PUTTS	COMMENTS
1						
2						
3						
4						
5						
6						
7						
8						
9						
TOTAL						
10						
11						
12						
13						
14						
15						
16						
17						
18						
TOTAL						

RESULT: _____ No. of EAGLES: _____ No. OF BIRDIES: _____   RESULT: _____ No. of EAGLES: _____ No. OF BIRDIES: _____

No. OF PARS: _____ No. OF BOGIES: _____ No. OF DOUBLE BOGIES: _____   No. OF PARS: _____ No. OF BOGIES: _____ No. OF DOUBLE BOGIES: _____

AREAS FOR IMPROVEMENT: _____   AREAS FOR IMPROVEMENT: _____

COURSE: _____ PAR: _____

DATE: _____ WEATHER CONDITIONS: _____

HOLE	PAR	SCORE	FAIRWAYS	GREENS	PUTTS	COMMENTS
1						
2						
3						
4						
5						
6						
7						
8						
9						
TOTAL						
10						
11						
12						
13						
14						
15						
16						
17						
18						
TOTAL						

RESULT: _____ No. of EAGLES: _____ No. OF BIRDIES: _____

No. OF PARS: _____ No. OF BOGIES: _____ No. OF DOUBLE BOGIES: _____

AREAS FOR IMPROVEMENT: _____

COURSE: _____ PAR: _____

DATE: _____ WEATHER CONDITIONS: _____

HOLE	PAR	SCORE	FAIRWAYS	GREENS	PUTTS	COMMENTS
1						
2						
3						
4						
5						
6						
7						
8						
9						
TOTAL						
10						
11						
12						
13						
14						
15						
16						
17						
18						
TOTAL						

RESULT: _____ No. of EAGLES: _____ No. OF BIRDIES: _____

No. OF PARS: _____ No. OF BOGIES: _____ No. OF DOUBLE BOGIES: _____

AREAS FOR IMPROVEMENT: _____

GREENS

17-18									
15-16									
13-14									
11-12									
9-10									
7-8									
5-6									
3-4									
1-2									
DATE									

FAIRWAYS

17-18									
15-16									
13-14									
11-12									
9-10									
7-8									
5-6									
3-4									
1-2									
DATE									

PUTTS

47-48									
45-46									
43-44									
41-42									
39-40									
37-38									
35-36									
33-34									
31-32									
29-30									
27-28									
25-26									
DATE									

SCORE

116-120									
111-115									
106-110									
101-105									
96-100									
91-95									
86-90									
81-85									
76-80									
71-75									
65-70									
DATE									

BUNKER PLAY

Draw three circles in the sand,
about a hand-span in diameter.
Your aim is to "throw" sand
onto the green.

It is important in a bunker
shot to follow through as
you would with your
normal swing.

Following through will ensure
that the sand lying in front of,
under and behind your ball is
blasted out and that your ball
goes with it.

COURSE: _____ PAR: _____   COURSE: _____ PAR: _____

DATE: _____ WEATHER CONDITIONS: _____   DATE: _____ WEATHER CONDITIONS: _____

HOLE	PAR	SCORE	FAIRWAYS	GREENS	PUTTS	COMMENTS
1						
2						
3						
4						
5						
6						
7						
8						
9						
TOTAL						
10						
11						
12						
13						
14						
15						
16						
17						
18						
TOTAL						

HOLE	PAR	SCORE	FAIRWAYS	GREENS	PUTTS	COMMENTS
1						
2						
3						
4						
5						
6						
7						
8						
9						
TOTAL						
10						
11						
12						
13						
14						
15						
16						
17						
18						
TOTAL						

RESULT: _____ No. of EAGLES: _____ No. OF BIRDIES: _____   RESULT: _____ No. of EAGLES: _____ No. OF BIRDIES: _____

No. OF PARS: _____ No. OF BOGIES: _____ No. OF DOUBLE BOGIES: _____   No. OF PARS: _____ No. OF BOGIES: _____ No. OF DOUBLE BOGIES: _____

AREAS FOR IMPROVEMENT: _____   AREAS FOR IMPROVEMENT: _____

_____   _____

COURSE: _____ PAR: _____

DATE: _____ WEATHER CONDITIONS: _____

HOLE	PAR	SCORE	FAIRWAYS	GREENS	PUTTS	COMMENTS
1						
2						
3						
4						
5						
6						
7						
8						
9						
TOTAL						
10						
11						
12						
13						
14						
15						
16						
17						
18						
TOTAL						

RESULT:_____ No. of EAGLES: _____ No. OF BIRDIES: _____

No. OF PARS: _____ No. OF BOGIES:_____ No. OF DOUBLE BOGIES: _____

AREAS FOR IMPROVEMENT: _____

_____

COURSE: _____ PAR: _____

DATE: _____ WEATHER CONDITIONS: _____

HOLE	PAR	SCORE	FAIRWAYS	GREENS	PUTTS	COMMENTS
1						
2						
3						
4						
5						
6						
7						
8						
9						
TOTAL						
10						
11						
12						
13						
14						
15						
16						
17						
18						
TOTAL						

RESULT:_____ No. of EAGLES: _____ No. OF BIRDIES: _____

No. OF PARS: _____ No. OF BOGIES:_____ No. OF DOUBLE BOGIES: _____

AREAS FOR IMPROVEMENT: _____

_____

COURSE: _____ PAR: _____

DATE: _____ WEATHER CONDITIONS: _____

HOLE	PAR	SCORE	FAIRWAYS	GREENS	PUTTS	COMMENTS
1						
2						
3						
4						
5						
6						
7						
8						
9						
TOTAL						
10						
11						
12						
13						
14						
15						
16						
17						
18						
TOTAL						

RESULT: _____ No. of EAGLES: _____ No. OF BIRDIES: _____

No. OF PARS: _____ No. OF BOGIES: _____ No. OF DOUBLE BOGIES: _____

AREAS FOR IMPROVEMENT: _____

COURSE: _____ PAR: _____

DATE: _____ WEATHER CONDITIONS: _____

HOLE	PAR	SCORE	FAIRWAYS	GREENS	PUTTS	COMMENTS
1						
2						
3						
4						
5						
6						
7						
8						
9						
TOTAL						
10						
11						
12						
13						
14						
15						
16						
17						
18						
TOTAL						

RESULT: _____ No. of EAGLES: _____ No. OF BIRDIES: _____

No. OF PARS: _____ No. OF BOGIES: _____ No. OF DOUBLE BOGIES: _____

AREAS FOR IMPROVEMENT: _____

COURSE: _____ PAR: _____   COURSE: _____ PAR: _____

DATE: _____ WEATHER CONDITIONS: _____   DATE: _____ WEATHER CONDITIONS: _____

HOLE	PAR	SCORE	FAIRWAYS	GREENS	PUTTS	COMMENTS
1						
2						
3						
4						
5						
6						
7						
8						
9						
TOTAL						
10						
11						
12						
13						
14						
15						
16						
17						
18						
TOTAL						

HOLE	PAR	SCORE	FAIRWAYS	GREENS	PUTTS	COMMENTS
1						
2						
3						
4						
5						
6						
7						
8						
9						
TOTAL						
10						
11						
12						
13						
14						
15						
16						
17						
18						
TOTAL						

RESULT: _____ No. of EAGLES: _____ No. OF BIRDIES: _____   RESULT: _____ No. of EAGLES: _____ No. OF BIRDIES: _____

No. OF PARS: _____ No. OF BOGIES: _____ No. OF DOUBLE BOGIES: _____   No. OF PARS: _____ No. OF BOGIES: _____ No. OF DOUBLE BOGIES: _____

AREAS FOR IMPROVEMENT: _____   AREAS FOR IMPROVEMENT: _____

COURSE: _____ PAR: _____   COURSE: _____ PAR: _____

DATE: _____ WEATHER CONDITIONS:_____   DATE: _____ WEATHER CONDITIONS:_____

HOLE	PAR	SCORE	FAIRWAYS	GREENS	PUTTS	COMMENTS
1						
2						
3						
4						
5						
6						
7						
8						
9						
TOTAL						
10						
11						
12						
13						
14						
15						
16						
17						
18						
TOTAL						

HOLE	PAR	SCORE	FAIRWAYS	GREENS	PUTTS	COMMENTS
1						
2						
3						
4						
5						
6						
7						
8						
9						
TOTAL						
10						
11						
12						
13						
14						
15						
16						
17						
18						
TOTAL						

RESULT:_____ No. of EAGLES: _____ No. OF BIRDIES: _____   RESULT:_____ No. of EAGLES: _____ No. OF BIRDIES: _____

No. OF PARS: _____ No. OF BOGIES:_____ No. OF DOUBLE BOGIES: _____   No. OF PARS: _____ No. OF BOGIES:_____ No. OF DOUBLE BOGIES: _____

AREAS FOR IMPROVEMENT: _____   AREAS FOR IMPROVEMENT: _____

_____   _____

GREENS

17-18									
15-16									
13-14									
11-12									
9-10									
7-8									
5-6									
3-4									
1-2									
DATE									

FAIRWAYS

17-18									
15-16									
13-14									
11-12									
9-10									
7-8									
5-6									
3-4									
1-2									
DATE									

PUTTS

47-48									
45-46									
43-44									
41-42									
39-40									
37-38									
35-36									
33-34									
31-32									
29-30									
27-28									
25-26									
DATE									

SCORE

116-120									
111-115									
106-110									
101-105									
96-100									
91-95									
86-90									
81-85									
76-80									
71-75									
65-70									
DATE									

COURSE: _____ PAR: _____

DATE: _____ WEATHER CONDITIONS: _____

HOLE	PAR	SCORE	FAIRWAYS	GREENS	PUTTS	COMMENTS
1						
2						
3						
4						
5						
6						
7						
8						
9						
TOTAL						
10						
11						
12						
13						
14						
15						
16						
17						
18						
TOTAL						

RESULT: _____ No. of EAGLES: _____ No. OF BIRDIES: _____

No. OF PARS: _____ No. OF BOGIES: _____ No. OF DOUBLE BOGIES: _____

AREAS FOR IMPROVEMENT: _____

_____

COURSE: _____ PAR: _____

DATE: _____ WEATHER CONDITIONS: _____

HOLE	PAR	SCORE	FAIRWAYS	GREENS	PUTTS	COMMENTS
1						
2						
3						
4						
5						
6						
7						
8						
9						
TOTAL						
10						
11						
12						
13						
14						
15						
16						
17						
18						
TOTAL						

RESULT: _____ No. of EAGLES: _____ No. OF BIRDIES: _____

No. OF PARS: _____ No. OF BOGIES: _____ No. OF DOUBLE BOGIES: _____

AREAS FOR IMPROVEMENT: _____

_____

COURSE: _____ PAR: _____

DATE: _____ WEATHER CONDITIONS: _____

HOLE	PAR	SCORE	FAIRWAYS	GREENS	PUTTS	COMMENTS
1						
2						
3						
4						
5						
6						
7						
8						
9						
TOTAL						
10						
11						
12						
13						
14						
15						
16						
17						
18						
TOTAL						

RESULT:_____ No. of EAGLES: _____ No. OF BIRDIES: _____

No. OF PARS: _____ No. OF BOGIES:_____ No. OF DOUBLE BOGIES: _____

AREAS FOR IMPROVEMENT: _____

_____

COURSE: _____ PAR: _____

DATE: _____ WEATHER CONDITIONS: _____

HOLE	PAR	SCORE	FAIRWAYS	GREENS	PUTTS	COMMENTS
1						
2						
3						
4						
5						
6						
7						
8						
9						
TOTAL						
10						
11						
12						
13						
14						
15						
16						
17						
18						
TOTAL						

RESULT:_____ No. of EAGLES: _____ No. OF BIRDIES: _____

No. OF PARS: _____ No. OF BOGIES:_____ No. OF DOUBLE BOGIES: _____

AREAS FOR IMPROVEMENT: _____

_____

COURSE: _____ PAR: _____   COURSE: _____ PAR: _____

DATE: _____ WEATHER CONDITIONS: _____   DATE: _____ WEATHER CONDITIONS: _____

HOLE	PAR	SCORE	FAIRWAYS	GREENS	PUTTS	COMMENTS
1						
2						
3						
4						
5						
6						
7						
8						
9						
TOTAL						
10						
11						
12						
13						
14						
15						
16						
17						
18						
TOTAL						

HOLE	PAR	SCORE	FAIRWAYS	GREENS	PUTTS	COMMENTS
1						
2						
3						
4						
5						
6						
7						
8						
9						
TOTAL						
10						
11						
12						
13						
14						
15						
16						
17						
18						
TOTAL						

RESULT:_____ No. of EAGLES: _____ No. OF BIRDIES: _____   RESULT:_____ No. of EAGLES: _____ No. OF BIRDIES: _____

No. OF PARS: _____ No. OF BOGIES:_____ No. OF DOUBLE BOGIES: _____   No. OF PARS: _____ No. OF BOGIES:_____ No. OF DOUBLE BOGIES: _____

AREAS FOR IMPROVEMENT: _____   AREAS FOR IMPROVEMENT: _____

_____   _____

COURSE: _____ PAR: _____

DATE: _____ WEATHER CONDITIONS: _____

HOLE	PAR	SCORE	FAIRWAYS	GREENS	PUTTS	COMMENTS
1						
2						
3						
4						
5						
6						
7						
8						
9						
TOTAL						
10						
11						
12						
13						
14						
15						
16						
17						
18						
TOTAL						

RESULT: _____ No. of EAGLES: _____ No. OF BIRDIES: _____

No. OF PARS: _____ No. OF BOGIES: _____ No. OF DOUBLE BOGIES: _____

AREAS FOR IMPROVEMENT: _____

_____

COURSE: _____ PAR: _____

DATE: _____ WEATHER CONDITIONS: _____

HOLE	PAR	SCORE	FAIRWAYS	GREENS	PUTTS	COMMENTS
1						
2						
3						
4						
5						
6						
7						
8						
9						
TOTAL						
10						
11						
12						
13						
14						
15						
16						
17						
18						
TOTAL						

RESULT: _____ No. of EAGLES: _____ No. OF BIRDIES: _____

No. OF PARS: _____ No. OF BOGIES: _____ No. OF DOUBLE BOGIES: _____

AREAS FOR IMPROVEMENT: _____

COURSE: _____ PAR: _____

DATE: _____ WEATHER CONDITIONS: _____

HOLE	PAR	SCORE	FAIRWAYS	GREENS	PUTTS	COMMENTS
1						
2						
3						
4						
5						
6						
7						
8						
9						
TOTAL						
10						
11						
12						
13						
14						
15						
16						
17						
18						
TOTAL						

RESULT: _____ No. of EAGLES: _____ No. OF BIRDIES: _____

No. OF PARS: _____ No. OF BOGIES: _____ No. OF DOUBLE BOGIES: _____

AREAS FOR IMPROVEMENT: _____

COURSE: _____ PAR: _____

DATE: _____ WEATHER CONDITIONS: _____

HOLE	PAR	SCORE	FAIRWAYS	GREENS	PUTTS	COMMENTS
1						
2						
3						
4						
5						
6						
7						
8						
9						
TOTAL						
10						
11						
12						
13						
14						
15						
16						
17						
18						
TOTAL						

RESULT: _____ No. of EAGLES: _____ No. OF BIRDIES: _____

No. OF PARS: _____ No. OF BOGIES: _____ No. OF DOUBLE BOGIES: _____

AREAS FOR IMPROVEMENT: _____

GREENS

DATE									
17-18									
15-16									
13-14									
11-12									
9-10									
7-8									
5-6									
3-4									
1-2									

FAIRWAYS

DATE									
17-18									
15-16									
13-14									
11-12									
9-10									
7-8									
5-6									
3-4									
1-2									

PUTTS

DATE									
47-48									
45-46									
43-44									
41-42									
39-40									
37-38									
35-36									
33-34									
31-32									
29-30									
27-28									
25-26									

SCORE

DATE									
116-120									
111-115									
106-110									
101-105									
96-100									
91-95									
86-90									
81-85									
76-80									
71-75									
65-70									

THE PUTTING LADDER

Place five balls half a putter length apart on the same line. Starting from the ball nearest the hole, your goal is to hole all five putts in a row. If you lose your concentration and miss one, you have to restart the exercise.

STAR DRILL

Place five balls evenly spaced one metre around the hole. Make sure you complete your putting routine for each putt as you would on the golf course. Become competent at this distance and watch your putting score decrease.

COURSE:	PAR:

DATE: _____ WEATHER CONDITIONS: _____

HOLE	PAR	SCORE	FAIRWAYS	GREENS	PUTTS	COMMENTS
1						
2						
3						
4						
5						
6						
7						
8						
9						
TOTAL						
10						
11						
12						
13						
14						
15						
16						
17						
18						
TOTAL						

RESULT:_____ No. of EAGLES: _____ No. OF BIRDIES: _____

No. OF PARS: _____ No. OF BOGIES:_____ No. OF DOUBLE BOGIES: _____

AREAS FOR IMPROVEMENT: _____

_____

COURSE:	PAR:

DATE: _____ WEATHER CONDITIONS: _____

HOLE	PAR	SCORE	FAIRWAYS	GREENS	PUTTS	COMMENTS
1						
2						
3						
4						
5						
6						
7						
8						
9						
TOTAL						
10						
11						
12						
13						
14						
15						
16						
17						
18						
TOTAL						

RESULT:_____ No. of EAGLES: _____ No. OF BIRDIES: _____

No. OF PARS: _____ No. OF BOGIES:_____ No. OF DOUBLE BOGIES: _____

AREAS FOR IMPROVEMENT: _____

_____

COURSE: _____ PAR: _____   COURSE: _____ PAR: _____

DATE: _____ WEATHER CONDITIONS:_____   DATE: _____ WEATHER CONDITIONS:_____

HOLE	PAR	SCORE	FAIRWAYS	GREENS	PUTTS	COMMENTS
1						
2						
3						
4						
5						
6						
7						
8						
9						
TOTAL						
10						
11						
12						
13						
14						
15						
16						
17						
18						
TOTAL						

HOLE	PAR	SCORE	FAIRWAYS	GREENS	PUTTS	COMMENTS
1						
2						
3						
4						
5						
6						
7						
8						
9						
TOTAL						
10						
11						
12						
13						
14						
15						
16						
17						
18						
TOTAL						

RESULT:_____ No. of EAGLES: _____ No. OF BIRDIES: _____   RESULT:_____ No. of EAGLES: _____ No. OF BIRDIES: _____

No. OF PARS: _____ No. OF BOGIES:_____ No. OF DOUBLE BOGIES: _____   No. OF PARS: _____ No. OF BOGIES:_____ No. OF DOUBLE BOGIES: _____

AREAS FOR IMPROVEMENT: _____   AREAS FOR IMPROVEMENT: _____

COURSE: _____ PAR: _____ COURSE: _____ PAR: _____

DATE: _____ WEATHER CONDITIONS: _____ DATE: _____ WEATHER CONDITIONS: _____

HOLE	PAR	SCORE	FAIRWAYS	GREENS	PUTTS	COMMENTS
1						
2						
3						
4						
5						
6						
7						
8						
9						
TOTAL						
10						
11						
12						
13						
14						
15						
16						
17						
18						
TOTAL						

HOLE	PAR	SCORE	FAIRWAYS	GREENS	PUTTS	COMMENTS
1						
2						
3						
4						
5						
6						
7						
8						
9						
TOTAL						
10						
11						
12						
13						
14						
15						
16						
17						
18						
TOTAL						

RESULT: _____ No. of EAGLES: _____ No. OF BIRDIES: _____

No. OF PARS: _____ No. OF BOGIES: _____ No. OF DOUBLE BOGIES: _____

AREAS FOR IMPROVEMENT: _____

RESULT: _____ No. of EAGLES: _____ No. OF BIRDIES: _____

No. OF PARS: _____ No. OF BOGIES: _____ No. OF DOUBLE BOGIES: _____

AREAS FOR IMPROVEMENT: _____

COURSE: _____ PAR: _____ COURSE: _____ PAR: _____

DATE: _____ WEATHER CONDITIONS: _____ DATE: _____ WEATHER CONDITIONS: _____

HOLE	PAR	SCORE	FAIRWAYS	GREENS	PUTTS	COMMENTS
1						
2						
3						
4						
5						
6						
7						
8						
9						
TOTAL						
10						
11						
12						
13						
14						
15						
16						
17						
18						
TOTAL						

HOLE	PAR	SCORE	FAIRWAYS	GREENS	PUTTS	COMMENTS
1						
2						
3						
4						
5						
6						
7						
8						
9						
TOTAL						
10						
11						
12						
13						
14						
15						
16						
17						
18						
TOTAL						

RESULT:_____ No. of EAGLES: _____ No. OF BIRDIES: _____

No. OF PARS: _____ No. OF BOGIES:_____ No. OF DOUBLE BOGIES: _____

AREAS FOR IMPROVEMENT: _____

RESULT:_____ No. of EAGLES: _____ No. OF BIRDIES: _____

No. OF PARS: _____ No. OF BOGIES:_____ No. OF DOUBLE BOGIES: _____

AREAS FOR IMPROVEMENT: _____

COURSE: _____ PAR: _____

DATE: _____ WEATHER CONDITIONS: _____

HOLE	PAR	SCORE	FAIRWAYS	GREENS	PUTTS	COMMENTS
1						
2						
3						
4						
5						
6						
7						
8						
9						
TOTAL						
10						
11						
12						
13						
14						
15						
16						
17						
18						
TOTAL						

RESULT:_____ No. of EAGLES: _____ No. OF BIRDIES: _____

No. OF PARS: _____ No. OF BOGIES:_____ No. OF DOUBLE BOGIES: _____

AREAS FOR IMPROVEMENT: _____

_____

COURSE: _____ PAR: _____

DATE: _____ WEATHER CONDITIONS: _____

HOLE	PAR	SCORE	FAIRWAYS	GREENS	PUTTS	COMMENTS
1						
2						
3						
4						
5						
6						
7						
8						
9						
TOTAL						
10						
11						
12						
13						
14						
15						
16						
17						
18						
TOTAL						

RESULT:_____ No. of EAGLES: _____ No. OF BIRDIES: _____

No. OF PARS: _____ No. OF BOGIES:_____ No. OF DOUBLE BOGIES: _____

AREAS FOR IMPROVEMENT: _____

_____

GREENS

17-18									
15-16									
13-14									
11-12									
9-10									
7-8									
5-6									
3-4									
1-2									
DATE									

FAIRWAYS

17-18									
15-16									
13-14									
11-12									
9-10									
7-8									
5-6									
3-4									
1-2									
DATE									

PUTTS

47-48									
45-46									
43-44									
41-42									
39-40									
37-38									
35-36									
33-34									
31-32									
29-30									
27-28									
25-26									
DATE									

SCORE

116-120									
111-115									
106-110									
101-105									
96-100									
91-95									
86-90									
81-85									
76-80									
71-75									
65-70									
DATE									

COURSE: _____ PAR: _____

DATE: _____ WEATHER CONDITIONS: _____

HOLE	PAR	SCORE	FAIRWAYS	GREENS	PUTTS	COMMENTS
1						
2						
3						
4						
5						
6						
7						
8						
9						
TOTAL						
10						
11						
12						
13						
14						
15						
16						
17						
18						
TOTAL						

RESULT: _____ No. of EAGLES: _____ No. OF BIRDIES: _____

No. OF PARS: _____ No. OF BOGIES: _____ No. OF DOUBLE BOGIES: _____

AREAS FOR IMPROVEMENT: _____

_____

COURSE: _____ PAR: _____

DATE: _____ WEATHER CONDITIONS: _____

HOLE	PAR	SCORE	FAIRWAYS	GREENS	PUTTS	COMMENTS
1						
2						
3						
4						
5						
6						
7						
8						
9						
TOTAL						
10						
11						
12						
13						
14						
15						
16						
17						
18						
TOTAL						

RESULT: _____ No. of EAGLES: _____ No. OF BIRDIES: _____

No. OF PARS: _____ No. OF BOGIES: _____ No. OF DOUBLE BOGIES: _____

AREAS FOR IMPROVEMENT: _____

COURSE: _____ PAR: _____   COURSE: _____ PAR: _____

DATE: _____ _____ WEATHER CONDITIONS: _____   DATE: _____ WEATHER CONDITIONS: _____

HOLE	PAR	SCORE	FAIRWAYS	GREENS	PUTTS	COMMENTS
1						
2						
3						
4						
5						
6						
7						
0						
9						
TOTAL						
10						
11						
12						
13						
14						
15						
16						
17						
18						
TOTAL						

HOLE	PAR	SCORE	FAIRWAYS	GREENS	PUTTS	COMMENTS
1						
2						
3						
4						
5						
6						
7						
8						
9						
TOTAL						
10						
11						
12						
13						
14						
15						
16						
17						
18						
TOTAL						

RESULT:_____ No. of EAGLES: _____ No. OF BIRDIES: _____   RESULT:_____ No. of EAGLES: _____ No. OF BIRDIES: _____

No. OF PARS: _____ No. OF BOGIES: _____ No. OF DOUBLE BOGIES: _____   No. OF PARS: _____ No. OF BOGIES: _____ No. OF DOUBLE BOGIES: _____

AREAS FOR IMPROVEMENT: _____   AREAS FOR IMPROVEMENT: _____

COURSE: _____ PAR: _____

DATE: _____ WEATHER CONDITIONS: _____

HOLE	PAR	SCORE	FAIRWAYS	GREENS	PUTTS	COMMENTS
1						
2						
3						
4						
5						
6						
7						
8						
9						
TOTAL						
10						
11						
12						
13						
14						
15						
16						
17						
18						
TOTAL						

RESULT:_____ No. of EAGLES: _____ No. OF BIRDIES: _____

No. OF PARS: _____ No. OF BOGIES:_____ No. OF DOUBLE BOGIES: _____

AREAS FOR IMPROVEMENT: _____

_____

COURSE: _____ PAR: _____

DATE: _____ WEATHER CONDITIONS: _____

HOLE	PAR	SCORE	FAIRWAYS	GREENS	PUTTS	COMMENTS
1						
2						
3						
4						
5						
6						
7						
8						
9						
TOTAL						
10						
11						
12						
13						
14						
15						
16						
17						
18						
TOTAL						

RESULT:_____ No. of EAGLES: _____ No. OF BIRDIES: _____

No. OF PARS: _____ No. OF BOGIES:_____ No. OF DOUBLE BOGIES: _____

AREAS FOR IMPROVEMENT: _____

COURSE: _____ _____PAR: _____

DATE: _____WEATHER CONDITIONS: _____

HOLE	PAR	SCORE	FAIRWAYS	GREENS	PUTTS	COMMENTS
1						
2						
3						
4						
5						
6						
7						
8						
9						
TOTAL						
10						
11						
12						
13						
14						
15						
16						
17						
18						
TOTAL						

RESULT:_____No. of EAGLES: _____No. OF BIRDIES: _____

No. OF PARS: _____No. OF BOGIES:_____No. OF DOUBLE BOGIES: _____

AREAS FOR IMPROVEMENT: _____

_____

COURSE: _____ _____PAR: _____

DATE: _____ _____WEATHER CONDITIONS:_____

HOLE	PAR	SCORE	FAIRWAYS	GREENS	PUTTS	COMMENTS
1						
2						
3						
4						
5						
6						
7						
8						
9						
TOTAL						
10						
11						
12						
13						
14						
15						
16						
17						
18						
TOTAL						

RESULT:_____No. of EAGLES: _____No. OF BIRDIES: _____

No. OF PARS: _____No. OF BOGIES:_____No. OF DOUBLE BOGIES: _____

AREAS FOR IMPROVEMENT: _____

_____

COURSE: _____ PAR: _____

DATE: _____ WEATHER CONDITIONS: _____

HOLE	PAR	SCORE	FAIRWAYS	GREENS	PUTTS	COMMENTS
1						
2						
3						
4						
5						
6						
7						
8						
9						
TOTAL						
10						
11						
12						
13						
14						
15						
16						
17						
18						
TOTAL						

RESULT:_____ No. of EAGLES: _____ No. OF BIRDIES: _____

No. OF PARS: _____ No. OF BOGIES:_____ No. OF DOUBLE BOGIES: _____

AREAS FOR IMPROVEMENT: _____

_____

COURSE: _____ PAR: _____

DATE: _____ WEATHER CONDITIONS: _____

HOLE	PAR	SCORE	FAIRWAYS	GREENS	PUTTS	COMMENTS
1						
2						
3						
4						
5						
6						
7						
8						
9						
TOTAL						
10						
11						
12						
13						
14						
15						
16						
17						
18						
TOTAL						

RESULT:_____ No. of EAGLES: _____ No. OF BIRDIES: _____

No. OF PARS: _____ No. OF BOGIES:_____ No. OF DOUBLE BOGIES: _____

AREAS FOR IMPROVEMENT: _____

_____

GREENS

17-18									
15-16									
13-14									
11-12									
9-10									
7-8									
5-6									
3-4									
1-2									
DATE									

FAIRWAYS

17-18									
15-16									
13-14									
11-12									
9-10									
7-8									
5-6									
3-4									
1-2									
DATE									

PUTTS

47-48									
45-46									
43-44									
41-42									
39-40									
37-38									
35-36									
33-34									
31-32									
29-30									
27-28									
25-26									
DATE									

SCORE

116-120									
111-115									
106-110									
101-105									
96-100									
91-95									
86-90									
81-85									
76-80									
71-75									
65-70									
DATE									

PGA TOUR – Final 1999 Statistics

ALL AROUND LEADERS

The All Around Leaders statistic is computed by totaling a player's rank in each of the following statistics: Scoring Leaders, Putting Leaders, Eagle Leaders, Birdie Leaders, Sand Saves, Greens in Regulation, Driving Leaders, and Driving Accuracy.

Rank	Name	Events	Stat
1	Tiger Woods	21	120
2	Phil Mickelson	23	268
T3	David Duval	21	277
T3	Vijay Singh	29	277
5	Davis Love III	23	320
6	Kirk Triplett	26	349
7	Chris Perry	31	352
8	Dennis Paulson	28	359
9	Hal Sutton	25	365
10	Jonathan Kaye	32	372

SCORING LEADERS

Scoring Leaders is a weighted scoring average which takes the stroke average of the field into account. The statistic is computed by taking a player's total strokes for the year, adding an adjustment figure, and dividing by the total rounds played for the year. The adjustment figure is computed by determining the stroke average of the field for each round played. This average is subtracted from par to create an adjustment figure for each round. A player accumulates these adjustment figures for each round he participates in.

Rank	Name	Rounds	Stat
1	Tiger Woods	75	68.43
2	David Duval	74	69.17
3	Davis Love III	78	69.37
4	Justin Leonard	104	69.59
5	Hal Sutton	90	69.66
6	Jim Furyk	96	69.67
7	Nick Price	62	69.75
8	Vijay Singh	101	69.83
T9	Dudley Hart	88	69.98
T9	Payne Stewart	68	69.98

PUTTING LEADERS
(average strokes per hole)

Measures putting performance on greens hit in regulation.
For each green hit in regulation the total number of putts are
divided by the number of greens hit in regulation. By using
greens hit in regulation we are able to eliminate the effects
of chipping close and one putting in the computation.

EAGLE LEADERS

Eagle Leaders is the average number of holes between
each eagle.

Rank	Name	Rounds	Stat	Rank	Name	Rounds	Stat
1	Brad Faxon	63	1.723	1	Vijay Singh	101	104.8
2	Payne Stewart	68	1.726	2	Craig Barlow	85	117.7
3	Frank Lickliter	104	1.730	3	Carlos Franco	69	120.6
4	Scott McCarron	88	1.735	4	Harrison Frazar	96	123.4
5	Skip Kendall	105	1.737	5	David Toms	103	123.6
6	Steve Stricker	69	1.739	6	Jonathan Kaye	108	129.6
7	Lee Janzen	85	1.745	7	Joe Ogilvie	92	138.0
T8	Dennis Paulson	103	1.747	8	Ted Tryba	110	138.9
T8	Loren Roberts	89	1.747	9	Chris Smith	78	140.4
10	David Duval	74	1.748	10	John Daly	63	141.8

GREENS IN REGULATION

Greens in Regulation is the percentage of time a player was able to hit the green in regulation (greens hit in regulation/ holes played). A green is considered hit in regulation if any part of the ball is touching the putting surface and the number of strokes taken is 2 or less than par.

SAND SAVES
(percentage)

Sand Saves is the percentage of time a player was able to get up and down once in a greenside sand bunker. This up and down is computed regardless of score on the hole.

Rank	Name	Rounds	Stat
1	Tiger Woods	75	71.4
2	Joe Durant	79	70.3
T3	David Duval	74	69.4
T3	Duffy Waldorf	90	69.4
T5	Stephen Ames	55	69.2
T5	Chris Perry	120	69.2
7	Hal Sutton	90	69.1
8	Robert Allenby	84	69.0
T9	Fred Funk	118	68.9
T9	Kenny Perry	82	68.9

Rank	Name	Rounds	Stat
1	Jeff Sluman	111	67.3
2	David Frost	83	64.9
3	Corey Pavin	82	63.2
4	Greg Chalmers	106	62.2
5	Justin Leonard	104	61.9
6	Mike Reid	75	61.7
7	Billy Andrade	88	61.6
8	Scott Hoch	99	61.1
9	Brian Watts	84	60.9
10	Alan Bratton	72	60.2

BIRDIE LEADERS
(average per round)

Birdie Leaders is the average number of birdies made per round played.

DRIVING DISTANCE
(average yards per drive)

Driving Distance is the average number of yards per measured drive. Driving distance is measured on two holes per round. Care is taken to select two holes which face in opposite direction to counteract the effects of wind. Drives are measured to the point they come to rest regardless of whether they are in the fairway or not.

Rank	Name	Rounds	Stat
1	Tiger Woods	75	4.46
2	David Duval	74	4.24
3	Phil Mickelson	78	3.99
4	Davis Love III	78	3.93
5	Chris Perry	120	3.90
6	Scott McCarron	88	3.89
7	Frank Lickliter	104	3.88
8	Hal Sutton	90	3.87
9	Skip Kendall	105	3.83
10	Stephen Ames	55	3.80

Rank	Name	Rounds	Stat
1	John Daly	63	305.6
2	Chris Couch	72	295.8
3	Tiger Woods	75	293.1
4	Rory Sabbatini	78	292.7
5	Harrison Frazar	96	290.5
6	Chris Smith	78	287.2
T7	Barry Cheesman	97	287.1
T7	Scott McCarron	88	287.1
9	David Duval	74	286.8
10	Dennis Paulson	103	286.3

DRIVING ACCURACY
(percentage)

Driving Accuracy is the percentage of time a player is able to hit the fairway with his tee shot.

Rank	Name	Rounds	Stat
1	Fred Funk	118	80.2
2	Olin Browne	80	78.7
3	Joe Durant	79	78.6
T4	Corey Pavin	82	77.4
T4	Mike Reid	75	77.4
T4	Loren Roberts	89	77.4
7	Larry Mize	70	77.2
T8	Scott Gump	95	77.0
T8	Jeff Maggert	82	77.0
10	Pete Jordan	90	76.0

TOTAL DRIVING

Total Driving is computed by totalling a player's rank in both driving distance and driving accuracy.

Rank	Name	Events	Stat
1	Tiger Woods	21	52
2	Perry Moss	22	66
3	Hal Sutton	25	67
T4	Kenny Perry	26	71
T4	Kirk Triplett	26	71
T4	Grant Waite	31	71
T7	David Duval	21	77
T7	Davis Love III	23	77
9	Robert Allenby	27	94
10	Bill Glasson	24	97

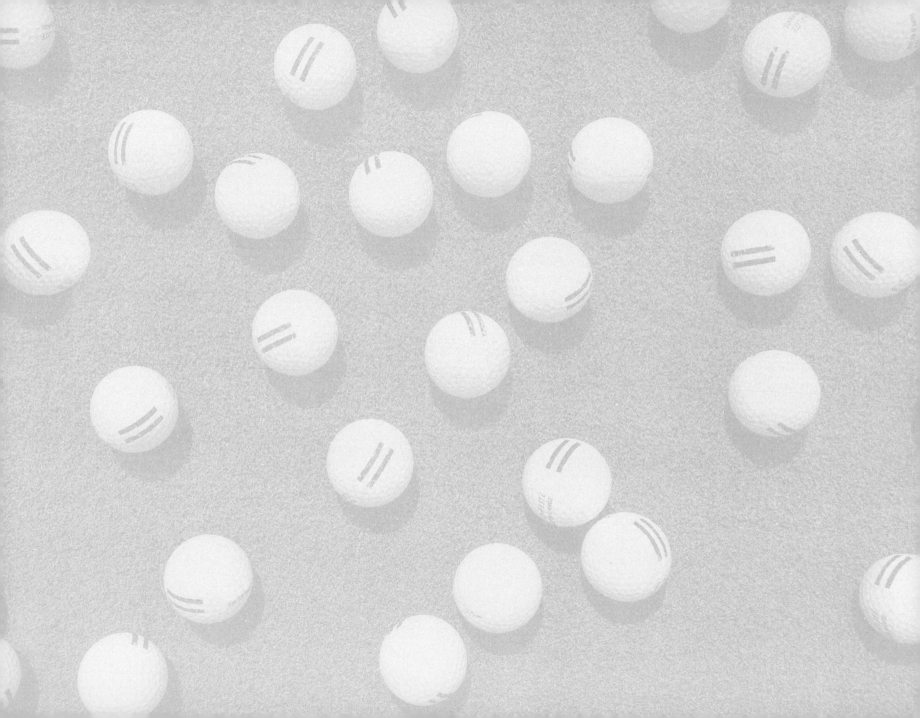

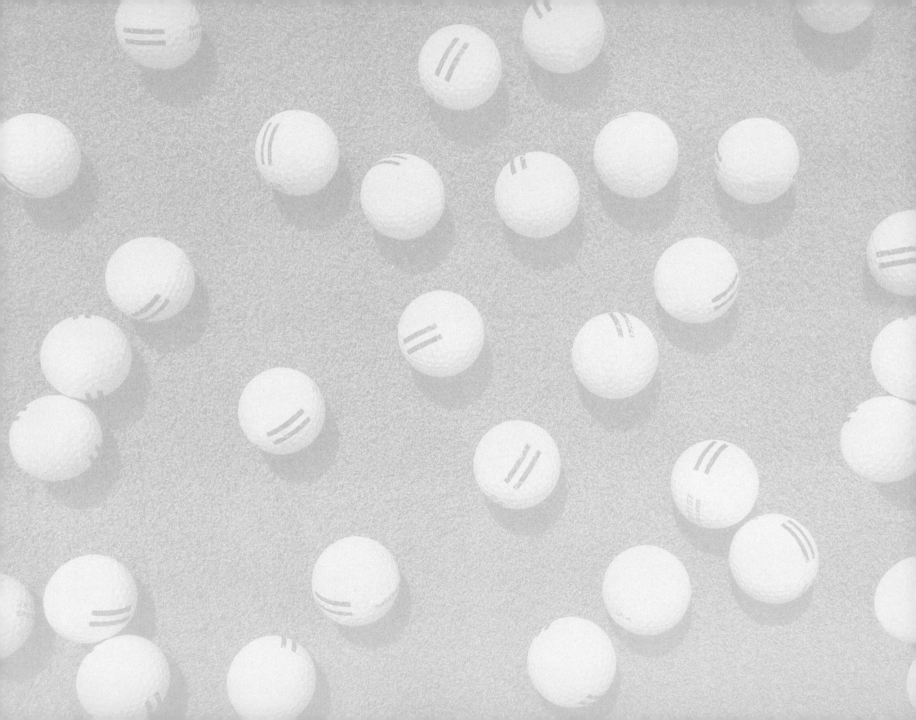